JOURNEY OF A SURVIVOR

PANDEMIC ERA

DARYL . J . R

To the entire world

For bearing such a heavy loss and still standing tall. This is quite short, maybe too extra for some but I belive, it is enough.

Contents

Prologue

Suffering is part of life, sure sometimes some suffer too much. Needless to say, people always take relationships for granted. This could be life telling us to cherish each other more. Forgiveness was and forever will be one of hardest humane thing that can be done. Meaning of life, now that is always a question. I hereby conclude through my book that life has no meaning but only one purpose i.e. to live.

CHAPTER ONE

The Beginning

24 March 2020, the day that shocked us; all the Indians, to go under 21 days of lockdown. Without proper preparations we went into hiding in our own houses with our family as rats, what could be done? It was dangerous to even take a step outside the house, even to breathe. Such was our fear during the first 7 days of the lockdown, due to the deadly virus i.e. the new topic of the media and the press.

My name is Joey Rodrigues, I am a Goan chef working in my own restaurant, in a blooming village called Colva. In my house there is non other than me, my wife Sana, my only son Joseph and my pet dog Michael.

Things have been tough ever since the first corona virus outbreak. Me and my wife were super cautions all the time, surviving for the first few days. The Government had already gave permissions for ration shops as well as groceries shops to be open during lockdown days so we had nothing to worry.

I was relieved to finally be able to take fresh air but wrong again, I could take all the air but by wearing a mask, which was absolutly suffocating. Right now bringing in suplies was my first concern. At first, home delivered food felt the right thing but my wife exaggerated, saying that maybe what if the delivery guy was infected, so I had to do it myself. I wouldn't say I didn't enjoy it as I met my neighbours on the way.

I knew that life will never be the same ever again. My son on the other part was in one way, nothing else but botherless, I could say that he cared less of the situation. I could not blame him, it was his age. He was to answer his 10th standard boared exams and boy wasn't he the happiest in the lockdown, reminded me of my childhood days but I did felt pity, as his could get ruined.

But the day did come for my son to answer his exams which was on 20 May 2020. It's good my son got some lockdown time to revise his subjets as he attained a good score of 75%. We were all happy but as things were, celebration was not meant to be.

People had to be carefull at the time. If they even coughed like for three times, they were harshly discriminated. There was an incident where a vegetable seller in my neighbourhood was found coughing for only two or three times and people started assuming him and his family as the infected. He and his family were tested negative but were still crticised, which led to rumors and than the closure of his grocery shop.

Soon the cases started rising, they numbered almost in the millions. People from the press had already got the name such as 'The Corona Virus'and 'The Covid-19' from the scientists.

Whatsapp messages and videos from many people started spreading about prevention, some messages were even about the cure for the virus, well I was about to belive them as such, when docters shared their views such as saying that people should not belive such kind of fake news as without testing, people cannot call themselves or others corona positive. Docters even stated that the virus has fever and cold like symtoms and but fake messages do spread like wildfire to such an extent that people said that there is no such virus.

Media went corrupt, right from the core. They said that the root cause of the virus was the people of China and the Chinese Government. The scientists gave an awesome theory saying that the virus evolved from bats and the reason people got it was because they ate some bat soup and I was really surprised. Well, I have been working as a cook for years ever since I was an 18 year old. I never made or ate bat soup but I can say one thing about it, that virus caused by a soup is hilairious, so whats next, death by eating rice or by noodles? That was my laugh for weeks and is still now is a good joke that I came up with at the moment.

I never travelled outside India, not even outside my lovely Goa. But from what I saw on the news people who left India are coming back via flights, they left India saying that India is not a good country to live in, than why ? Why do they return ?

Well I guess they have understood their country's worth. That is what I thought but guess I was wrong, they came back because India was providing better care to their citizens than the other countries or so was their reason.

As number of cases gave a rise so did the the number of deaths. Thousands of people died in this plague of the 21st Century which reached to a million by July.

People lost their sons, daughters, fathers, mothers and so many people whom they loved. People started getting furious on the govenment but what could they do, they were new to the dangerous situation. The government had implemented a lot of rules for safety but none followed them, epecially the youth. There are cases where the same youth were tested positive and were immediately taken to be hospitalised.

As time went by, the situations strated becoming worse and worse, I was terrified to even take a step outside my house even for 2 minutes. Even though being traped inside, I spent a lot of time with my family, I learned to connect with everyone and everything, I also had a lot of time to my self, to think and improvise. After months of less exercise, I was becoming fatter and fatter, gaining a lot of weight. Yes, the lockdown has its good effects but there are also those effects wherein you lose yourself.

I slowly started turning into a lunatic. I was once a humble family loving guy slowly turning into a lazy, news addicted guy. I could not live without news. Me and my son were having constant fights like never before, I was turning into a monster. My words were of that of a lazy person and of a verbal abuser, I realised it when I took a look at myself, in thoughts, asking myself, what I was and what I had become.

The media does have negitive effect on the minds of everyone who was watching news, little did I know that not only me but everyone in my neighbourhood were in the same situation. All my friends were affected with a new deadly virus, the one you get by watching the news and media, I thanked God almighty that I realised at the right moment.

I wanted to overcome my news addiction, which was absolutely difficult. I am about 45 years of age and at this age destroying a habit is far difficult than when I was a kid but my son helped me when I needed it the the most.

What my son advisd me was not to destroy a habit but to replace it. Guess what, it did work better than ever. I started getting back into shape by exercising, lost weight, started getting active, it did take me some months but it was worth it.

The thing about chefs like me is that we like to cook only in our workplace but not at home, but since I was at home I had to put my skills to practise or I might have gotten out of touch. I did not stop watching news but watched less, only at free time.

I did show off my skills to my wife, she was stunned but also jealous, as I was better than her. I guess I had to show her who was the real boss in cooking was. I did teach my son as well and he too became an expert, I must say that my son inherited my cooking skills; awesome genes. I realised that I can either better myself or spoil myself , I should make the best out of my free time.

At one time we were scared to learn that our neighbour, Mr.Fernandes, an 80 year old was tested positive, along with his family. They were immediately hospitalised, it's a good thing that we were not in contact with him or his family.

After 2 months we got the news that the old man sadly passed away but the rest of the family survived and were at last tested negative. Enrique, who is Mr.Fernandes son, my good friend shared his experience in the corona positive ward.

He stated that at first he thought everything would go smoothly, untill the moment after they entered te hospital. When they entered the special ward it looked as if it was hell on earth where the enternal fire; the real torment on Earth itself was the virus and people were burning in that fire.

There are certain wards, he stated. According to him people were layed on beds, couging and suffocating. In the higher wards people were given oxygen by some kind device with an oxgygen mask, I guess it was a respirator.

The nationwide lockdown ended on 30 June 2020. To be precise, the lockdown was dived into 4 phases. The first phase which started in 25th March 2020 ended on 14th April 2020 for 21 days. The second phase started on 15th April 2020 which was a rough phase did end in some problems but it proved to be effect, it ended on 3rd May 2020 for 14 days. The third phase which stated on 4th May 2020,by then everyone was getting used to the nationwide lockdown but problem did arrive on poor people as they were runnig out of money. Neverthless, people did manage to make it through this phase which ended on 17th may 2020. The last, the fourth phase, which started on 18th May 2020. I could say that people were eager to celebrate the end of lockdown as I too was waiting for it get over. It finally got over on 31st May 2020.

I felt like I got graduated from college and high school at the same time. The moment, the day it ended I became a kid again I was about to run eurika from home but my son and wife controled me and brought me back to my senses. You must be wondering what kind of person would do that, the only crack enough person would be me as I was like that since childhood, fully energetic.

After lockdown, I started focusing on getting back on my knees, so I went back to my to my restaurant, trying to continue bussiness but I got a big shock that I needed to get my permit renued or else no continuity of businesss.

So I got my permits, but to my luck, no one was interseted in coming to restaurants, my wife scolded me, not to reopen the place but I guess I was a stubborn fool.

My income was because of the tourism industry, indeed my restaurant is famous among the tourists, my awesome cooking and best service attracted a lot of cutomers but I have to agree that the price was a bit high. But still, the bussiness used to go pretty great.......Yh, used to.

My restaurant was situated close to the beach, so the feeling of being in the restaurant with the sound of the rough but calming waves was awesome in it's own way. I always thanked God for what I got in life but I was also too proud, I used to look down on my fellow competitors. But now everything came down I guess not just me but everyone was suffering a huge loss. Thank God my wife was a Government employed official so I did have support.....Aaye! that doesn't mean that I'm dependent on my wife, I too can earn. Its a good thing that she had taken a leave from the office before the lockdown that she was able to be with us and boy, was I gratefull for that but now she had to resume work.

My wife started arguing and fighting with me about the restaurant, about the losses that we would have to cover if bussiness didn't go well but I had to be a stubborn asshole, so for half a month I kept the restaurant open and things were not going smooth so in the end I had to close it. My wife resumed her work and with nothing to do, I became a househusband, though it may sound embarrassing to many but for me, it was work which had to be done. I understood the burden which women go through i.e taking care of everything.

Meanwhile, my son who was at home doing nothing, finally, his online classes began and boy was I relived. He always was in a conner, doing nothing. Me and my wife thought that it would better to get him admitted in the nearby higher secondary school, so things started going smooth for my son.

It's a good thing I saved and collected a lot of money before lockdown. I am not simply a bussinessman for nothing. The motto of a bussinesman is to rip more profit and to save more. So yes even though I don't sound like it but I am pretty wealthy, little do my friends and neighbours know, not even my son. The only person who knows about it was my wife, but she doesn't brag about it to her friends and family, which is a quatlity that proves her good personallity, so I am always gratefull towards her as she is always a great wife, without her help i.e. basically her strictness.... I would have been lost all this time, so thank God for that (no shame in admitting it).

As my son's online classes started, I noticed that he was not giving his best.....forget it, he was not even trying. Infact, he was the modern zombie of the house.... eat, sleep, online classes.... repeat. Things do take a turn for the worst, he used to sleep a lot during class....I mean a lot and still he used to get quality sleep at night......I wonder whose habbit has he takken up from, definitely not mine. Oh boy, what should've be done to him. I feared that he might fail if the school decides to keep an exam soon.

Oh dear lord! Did my fears come true and that to, with a lot of intensity. The school did decided to keep an exam. My wife did have high hopes for our boy, I guess I should've told her about the boy's recklessnes but something stopped me maybe it was curiosity or the fact that I am afraid of my wife, clearly she is the fighting type.

My son did say that his exams went fine but I knew something was wrong, the results came in after a while, I was not surprised but my wife was absolutely shocked...... volcanic eruption 'bout to happen....don't know why, read further. My son failed his examinations something I did expect, I used to constantly warn my son but he never thought wisely, but now, he will start to take things seriously. If she wasn't busy in her work, she would have known.

During the entire lockdown, I went through a lot of changes and so did people. The people's current situations were not as good ours, when we were having such a pleasant time, people were selling their bikes, car and some with prices very low, but how could people start buying those things. I myself would not buy in this situation. Even though if I had money, it would still be unwise to spend high on vehicles.

I had to get back in bussiness, that was all in my mind. I did not care about other people's situation. All I cared was about kicking back up, but not now as I thought. My restaurant shall shine once more someday again.

My son did make my wife worry a lot, she started getting gray hair and gray hair in her early forty meant stress. You must be wondering how in those years is a person not to get gray hair. To be honest my wife did throw a tantrum after seeing her first gray hair as she exclaimed that the women in her family do not get gray hair until they reach their early fiftys and boy was my son in huge trouble, that is what I thought. But to my surprise, I found out that I was in trouble as I was strictly ordered by my wife to keep a keen eye on my son. I am just guiding my son to the right path, so it isn't a trouble...... maybe. My son was scared, he must have been. Even though I was loving, I was more stricker and I did not have a choice, I did not have the rule in the house as my wife did, trust me no one in the family wants to fight with my wife. So I had to obey her..... I hope you understand.

Some states had to go for state lockdown due to the number of rising cases but none were showing recoving rates as fast, but death rate was also low. The most affected states were Delhi, Maharastra, Bihar and Uttar Pradesh, I would'nt be that surprised as they were the states which had a high population number.....more the population, more the crime and definitely more number of diseases.

Due to the lockdown and the strict actions of the Government of Goa, the state became a green zone. But was meant only for a short period. There were rumors that some people have crossed the state border to come to Goa and that the Government has permitted those people. My son thought that this should not be a problem, as we discussing over the news. His thoughts were clean, thinking that we should reach our arms to everyone in need. Little did he know that sometimes the help you offer, leads you in trouble.

The people who crossed borders were questioned and sent for testing and were kept quarantined for some weeks, some were tested positive.

And so the virus started spreading again and green zone tag of Goa had finally came off and some few months it officially became a red zone. Why God, why ? I complained.

Two days later I went to shop for groceries and I saw a shopkeeper sneezing and coughing very badly several times. People immediately thought that he was infected and called the police. To be honest, I too thought the same but later on I got news from my friend who said that the seller was tested negative but was having a rough cold. It was the same situation as that of the vegetable seller. I thought that if a guy got suspected just from sneezing, then what about the ones who have actually recoverd? People might have treated them wrong.

Cases were on the rise and the talks about the cure or the vaccines finally started to make it's way to the top headlines. To be certain a vaccine takes at least three years to be fully tested, prepared and tried, but not this one.

The first ever vaccine for the corona virus was made in just mere months. Many people were spreading rumors saying that they had all planned it out and that the virus was a man made disaster. But still, why would the political leaders do it, their families too would have been caught in the virus....wouldn't they?

People are just saying whatever they feel without even thinking logically, saying that they did it to keep the population in balance. I thought if that's the case than we should shift to planet Mars instead, atleast there won't people who spread rumors. I saw a news of a begger turning himself in after 38 years since he comitted crime, it did sound familiar but where? Hmm. His face was covered... kinda familiar character.

As time went on by, people started to recover by continuing their jobs and their bussiness once again so I thought about continuing my bussiness once again but there was a problem, a grave one, my workers and my staff members of my restaurant found new places to work so the idea of continuing my restaurent was dropped for a while.

Time went on by, it seemed that the Government had taken control over everything and so my son's online classes were coming to an end and the time to go to school came too soon.

At first my son was thrilled to finally go to school but after a while his face suddenly turned sour. I tried to understand his behaviour, it's not that I didn't ask him about it, I did but he said that everything was fine. I was still doubtful on his sudden change of behaviour so I asked my wife and she told me the surprising truth. She said that his books were all incomplete and his teacher was a harsh and a strict one. So this is why he had turned on a sour look on his face. I guess this is one of the side effects of having online classes, students become reckless and stop taking notes and studying, this was the reason he failed in his first formative test.

I talked to my younger brother Edward on the phone and he said that his daughter and his two sons were caught up in the same mess, so my son was not the only boy in this world to do that. He concluded that classwork which was given at school were being given at home along with homework and due to boredom they escaped by faking network issues or asking their hardworking friends for notes after class, which got pilled up in the chats. He also stated that everyone is new to online classes so it might take a lot of time for students to get used to it, as they can bunk and escape which is an advantage that they did not have before the pandemic .

After listening to my brothers words, I realised that my boy too, is going through a lot, it is his fault due to his recklessness but since he was new to the situation I cannot blame him alone for this, as he too is a very young boy, who is still growing up, making new mistakes which is a part of his life.

Life went on by, my son and other students, whose work was incomplete got hammered by the teacher on the first offline day in school. In time he caught up with everything and made some new friends. Some of his old friends did enroll in the same school so it was good for him as he was not alone but the bad thing was that all the students were socially distant from each other, he felt a bit awkward but he slowly got used to it.

After some few months I finally got some qualified cooks to run my retaurant again, plus I did not want to remain a househusband forever. I too wanted to cook as it was my passion, I don't want to use my talent at home only and I thought it would be better......as my wife was jealous of me.... for I am a better cook than her so it's better to let her cook again.

Finally back on track. Now my restaurant will shine again. Some few days back the government decided to continue tourism activites again. It seems they too ran out of money but the Government also decided that all shops,markets,stores and restaurants to close at 8.00PM sharp. But I was okay with it since times were still rough.

CHAPTER TWO

Life's A Beautiful Mess

Life started to play tricks again. Just when things were going fine, the Government decided to keep a state lockdown in Goa. God was I furious, I just reopened my restaurant and here we go again. I guess the people of the Government are useless and still immature at this age but they did have a reason to do so, well I must not think negative without knowing proper.

The state recorded 418 fresh cases due to the disease. Goa chief minister said that the essential shops will be allowed to remain open from 7 AM to 3 PM during the covid-19 lockdown. The Government of Goa announced the next day that the state will be put under another lockdown till June 14 2021 in an attempt to curb the spread of the spread of the coronavirus (covid-19).

Till now Goa recorded 418 fresh cases of covid-19 and 13 new deaths due to the virus. These took the overall infection tally in the state to 159,811 while the death toll soared to 2,840. As many as 6,397 active cases of the virus on record while 1,162 recoveries took place the other day, taking the total numer of recoveries to 150,574. Man! I even heard that it might extend. Only God knows when this might get over, I wish it was all over but it ain't that simple.

Just when everything was going through my mind, an important friendly character flashed infront my eyes......he's gotta be in this book. How could I ever forget about the person. I quickly called my best friend Salvador, though he is quite a bit drunked, he is quite the humerous guy. After knowing his and his family's wellbeing, I quickly asked about.... Mr.Shan.

Both salvador and Mr.Shan lived close to each other and when I mean close, I really mean very close. Well.....for the intro, Mr.Shan was a homeless begger who used to sleep outside Salvador's house. Though he was never let inside the house, Salvador always let him sleep outside in his huge lushy green and beautiful garden but not for free, Mr.Shan had to give him 1,000 rupees as rent. Well now, you must be wondering; how can a begger who doesn't have enough to live by pay 1000 rupees.... that's kinda absurd, right?

Well even though he looked innocent and pityfull Mr.Shan was a bussinessman in disguise, how? Let me explain. Though he was a begger, by the month he used to collect at least 7000 rupees; a modern day begger. So he had nothing less though he had lost the physical strength but he never lost his expert brains, he never used it to make an honest living.

Mr.Shan wasn't born poor, though being 37 years older then me, I knew him quite well. He taught me each and everything I knew in bussiness and let me inform you, even till now his teachings have not failed me. He used to be a successfull bussiness man but he was abandoned by his family, truly sad how his closest abandoned him. He cursed his family for abandoning him and soon after a while he got bankrupt. All his property got sealed, all his money taken over by the Government.

The police started searching him but they never knew that he had started living his life as a beggar so they could not find him, very sad flash back right? Well, absolutely no! Always remember, the story depends on the narrator, it can also be a lie. Whatever flashbacks Mr.Shan used to tell the people, most of them where lies. People used to take pity on his lies and this is how he used to get a profit of more than 2000 ruppes of begged money (It's called bussiness) and how do I know they were lies? It's truly simple, though it may sound complicated. The story does indeed depend on the narrator but only the ones who witnessed everything knew the true story.

It goes like this.... Mr.Shan, though he was a bussinessman, he was as cruel as a rotten thief. He was wicked in each and every way possible, torturing his wife to death and beating up his children badly. His children always used to search for him in differnt liqour bars even though he was cruel, they loved him a lot. But in the end, he did not show any signs of ever changing himself, so in vain his children left him and there started his bad time.

But after his children left, he changed in some few years. I knew it because he used to tell how he regreted it all and only if he had one last chance of redoing his life, that he would have do it in an honest and a very loving way ever. He truly began to understand life. I guess people change over the time. This is how God works; a truly beautifull way, people realise in time. Love you God, you are truly awesome.

So I asked Salvador about his wellbeing and he gave me the shock of the time. It seems during lockdown Mr.Shan went blank, no one gave money to him though he begged a lot, true hardwork but no success and plus he couldn't give rent anymore, though Salvador was ready to still let him stay, there was another problem; food and water. Now Salvador's wife was not an easy going person, who was my sister, a true female brute. Her name is Maria, though her name sounds sweet but she is not. All the boys of my age used to fear her for a reason. Handsome boys of my time used to try their charm on her as she was the most beautiful girl in the entire village but most of them went to their homes, not in saddness, not in frustration but in pure agony and next to the doctor screaming in pain as she had the habbit of breaking the bones of those boys, she was a black belt martial artist.... truly feared among men and women.

My sister was also the sweetest person as well, this could be seen. Salvador my true best friend was the weakest and the most bullied person in the village. My sister used to protect him from all danger possible. In the movies it is different but in real life, things happen in the opposite way. Then how did they get along? Well you see they both loved each other a lot right from childhood, they did end up together. That is how I know my elder sister is very sweet.

By the way, I too am a champion, a black belt but in cooking and not fighting, my sister was always there for me as my bodyguard, not that I am proud of it but I sill own a lot to my sister who protected me from those bullies. To thank her! Cause no girl ever...... when I mean to say ever, I truly mean it..... ever came close to me! But thankfully, I found the right girl who was never afraid of my sister and surprisingly, she wasn't my sister's best friend either but her rival, her enemy. The best revenge on her as I can say, as both of them were black belts who never won against each other, the match always ended in a draw. I can safely say that my wife was also a brute, yes.... truly safely.

I never knew that there was someone equal to my sister until the day I saw her, truly awesome and stunning to the core. I coud never forget the day. After that day, I always observed and tried to find more info about her.

It turned out she was the quitest girl who used to sit at the cornor of her class and another shocking thing was every girl besides her true friends, used to try to bully her and the most shocking thing was that both my sister and that girl hated each other, some hidden past, both still hate each other though. Just like the 90s films I used to follow her to her house trying to sum up the courage to say hi but I was always nervous. One day she caught me red handed. Now don't think that she left me safe and sound. She very well knew that I was Maria's brother and thought that I was spying on her, so she beat me up real bad. Well even after that I still used to follow her, you could say that my love for her was very deeply rooted, as of now you must have realised me as a madman.

Thank God I could write great poetries and yeah I did.... poetries full of love and I was the emperor. Through my loving poetries I caught her attention and there, I graduated from life. News did spread to my sister who was furious but could not do a thing as our parents had no objection. Blesssed me...... a sweet devil.

Lets get back to the main part, as of now Mr.Shan was completely pennyless, he had nothing in his pockets. It seems that one day he suddenly disappered without a trace, nothing but a note at the door matt. It said, “Salvador, I don’t want to burden you and your wife. I have no ills thoughts but true and deep gratitude, it’s time for me to be a true man and admitt my sins and crimes, once and for all. Its been such a long road to this part of life, I did spent a lot of time with you and your family and I became a part of it as well. My selfishness did cost me a lot; my family, friends and my life. Farewell”.

Even though I was on phone, I was truly sad and worried for the guy, since he was my teacher in commerse, truly loved him as family.

“didn’t u know?’’.

“what?”. I asked.

“ he got arrested, he turned himself in the police months ago”.

If I do recall, there was a news about a man turning himself over to the police after 38 years who was now a begger..... Oops.

“oh”, I said, “yeah, though he became a good human being, talk about changes that take in time”.

After a while of refreshing memmories on the phone, we ended the chat.

Just when I kept the phone, I saw a newspaper on my desk. The newspaper was a few months old and there on the head lines; ‘Shah Habbie Azeb Nour(in short ‘Shan’) turned himself over after 38 years of being a begger. Who would have know......

It was quite a relief, why didn’t I read this newspaper months ago, whatever. As I continued reading, I read the judge’s name and I knew that it was him, the one person who I hated the most, my life-long-nemesis, ‘Michael .J. Fernandes’, no doubt it was him, after all he was the judge who presided the case. Also, he is a very good judge, I have to admit it though we hate each other, since he was quite good in judging me and everyone during my childhood days and especially my glory youthfull days. I still hate him a lot.

But we Goans are different, cause even though we hated each other, we were still in touch. We love our enemies, at least that’s what we show....they say, keep your friends close and your enemies closure. I called him and the starting conversation was something like this,

"Hey Joey, long time no voice, I was beginning to wonder that God had turned you mute." A true nemisis in heart.

"Brother I am still good, I hear you on the phone but for a long time I never saw your face. I guess after my sister punched your face, you became faceless..... What a pity."

"Now – now brother lets not refresh old memories. Cause if you do, you sure remember the time that I stole your first crush." This guy will never change.

I quickly went straight to the topic. " Have you heard of the man named Shah Habbie Azeb Nour".

"Nah, never heard of him".

" Are you serious!" I really got furious.

" Yeah man, I am." Giving me a quick reply.

"Did you not preside over the court for his case?"

"Whose?"

"Man enough with jokes. Do you not remember the case that you presided few months ago ?!"

"But whose ? If you don't tell the name, how will I know?"

"But I already told you!!". I was about to lose it

"Can you tell me the name again". I guess the person really lost all of his sense when my sister knocked him out with a punch.

"Shah Habbie Azeb Nour". I had to repeat.

"Wait, let me check". He takes a huge amount of time.

"Oh yes, the name is there on my diary, I guess I did preside over his case."

"Why? Whats the matter?"

"I wanna know everything about his case !" I insisted.

"But why? What does the case have something to do with you, I hope that you were not involved in this".

"Ah ! why do you have to ask too many question". This conversation was turning annoying, this is not a police inspection ! But it's not his fault for questioning me. I was desperate to know about 'my guru in commerse'.

"Nothing, I am involved in nothing". After I said these words, I felt that I have commited a sin as I did knew about Shan's real identity but it also would'nt make a difference either. So this is what people would call as 'a half lie'.

"Hey, you there?"

" Yeah I'm there". Just when I was deep in thought.

"So, why did you want to know about the case".

"It"s just that I had a deep friendship with the beggar". I replied.

"Which beggar are you talking about?"

"Baba, you are really annoying me. You nah!". O God, please bring his common sense back !

"Can you do one thing?"

"Yeah?"

'Go to hell'. That is what I wanted to say but since I have something known as decency, I said,

"Please collect all the information about the case. Let's talk about this tomorrow evening".

"Ok, take care then".

"You too" and I kept the phone.

" So what was your crush's name?"(someone from the back),

that someone turned out to be my doom... oops my wife.

"So.....?"

"Just a blast from the past". I replied .

Well, most wives do get curious but mine, let me off with a smile. People must know that the society in Goa is a female dominated, but when it comes to political control, I say we males have an upper hand. So my house husband day continued and suprisingly, I was getting used it. Plus, I was getting shreddded with six pack abbs. Guess being a house husband ain't that bad. I guess people who are single may not be that happy but me, I got the perfect partner.

The next day Michael called me. This time, we had a pretty smooth conversation. It turns out that Shan got shifted to a jail outside Goa, never to be seen again in this state by law. I asked him the name of the jail but he said that he can't tell as he was obliged only to share this personal information with his family and that Shan was safe and sound. Before finishing the call, I gave him a sweet and short poem,

"Hey brother, wanna listen to a poem ?"

"Sure, I wanna hear what you got."

'ANGER'

-If I had an axe, please don't flex
Damn you, I would definitely love to butcher you, T-rex
-If you think you had the tool
Don't forget, I am the one and only Big Bull
-If I was a preacher,
I would've slapped your face like an english teacher
-The last one will sting, it's the next biggest thing
-If I was your die-hard fan'
I would've literally roasted you like an omlete on the frying pan.

A very beautifull peom, don't you think."

"Why oh why are your poems so awesome?"

"cuz I'm the best". I replied. With this the conversation was over. I hung up the phone.

Life went on like a tsunami wave this time, taking everyone with it without any mercy nor pity, I guess it was a lesson for us all mankind to start taking stuff seriously. Life becomes valuable through our struggles,our difficuties and our gains. But this pandemic could be the biggest struggle of the current generation.

My boy underwent excessive hairfall, it was a clear sign of stress and lack of sleep. I felt anger and disappointment at the same time. Anger, I felt because of how poor the education system had become especialy during the pandemic and disappointment, I was disappionted in my son as he was not able to adapt quickly to the situation.

Yes, my boy had passed in his subject and move onto to 12th grade but I could say that he barely passed and was not happy about it. Though me and his mother tried to cheer him up, but only for some time. As if life had become unfair for my innocent boy. When you are a small child, you are taught that trying is good thing but in the future, trying does not matter but results do.

As I look at myself I too remember my struggles, sure they were not as many as his but were indeed like the second level of hell. Even though I was bright, I had a lot of problems such as verbally abusive dad who used to demotivate me each and everytime, I tried to do good. Guess my old man never understood me..... tough love was what my dad knew. Can't blame my dad for who he is. He's been though a lot of stuff. But my mother on the other hand was my saviour, if it hadn't been her then I would have given up my life a long time ago.

But here, my son even though he had both of us, still life had become the toughest for him. One thing that I tell him each and everytime is, 'that our struggle makes our life valuable and if life has has given you a hard punch, then stand up and give back a K.O to life, as you have what it takes to be the person who you want to be.' That's what I say to my boy.

We make our on destiny, everything is in our grasp, we just need to realise how important we are. My son never asked me for this life but I asked for him and my wife too agree, even though she kept him in her womb for nine months, she never treated my boy with bad attitude, but with infinite gratitude towards God. It's truly difficult but she does her parenting strickly and perfectly. If I had a daughter, I know that she would've turned as sweet as her mother.

Now it was the end of the year 2020. Very few people actaully celebrated christmass, I guess there were too many loses and many people grived as they had lost their loved ones even at christmass. People around the world very few in number celebrating christmass was quite the saddest view of my life till now.

A new year was about to begin and my boy's smile which I hadn't seen for a long time came back. As the new year begun, I felt like my boy knew exactly what to do. I was literally shocked when he told that he will definitely fire cuss words at all his teachers if they trouble him ever, in this new year... he told me that he did'nt give a damn 'bout his teachers and their cruel words, "no one will take away my self confidence and my self value ever again. I am alive and I will not keep quite at my teachers. I was truly shocked but I was and I said seriously, “no problem”. But my wife on the other hand, well she was not in a great mood after listening to his words, not to worry as I calmly explained to her and surprisingly she too agreed. Why won’t she, as she also had bad memmories due to her teachers so it was a ok situation. My son will never do that to his teachers but my wife could.....I won’t make the mistake of underestimating a women.

The state lockdown ended long back somewhere in the months of June and July 2020. But another problem had come up, the people that I had recruited had left and my restaurant need a lot of fixing and cleaning to do, “God!”, I was drowning in problems again and again and my devlish wife started teasing me. She teased me saying that you had a good time but I guess your time is up, for once she even sounded like the grim reaper and with that evil smileI knew that if my restaurant could not get started then bye-bye my cooking life and hello forever house- husband life? No.......no.....ah hell nah.

CHAPTER THREE

A Different Solution

My restaurant, I have to get it back on track or else I am done. I have to clean the place, it's a ruin now. If anyone enters it, then they will definitely gets creeps, pretty sure it looks like a haunted place now. Before fixing and cleaning, I have to check the damage that may have taken place during my absesnce. The moment I entered the place a strange wind flew against me. Yes, my restaurant now looks eaxctly a haunted place, at the moment I kept my right foot on the place, I saw my restaurants greatest enemy, it's life-long nemisis! "The Rat".

It was a huge one. The moment I saw it going to my kitchen, I saw my restaurants future going along with it's tail, enough to give me a cardiac arrest. God and as I followed it the kitchen, gave me my life's biggest horror yet. It was a rat coloney; infestation, enough to get me paralysed for life. I fell right on the floor, guess I almost lost my purpose for my cooking.

The next thing I remember, is my son waking me up and a gorgeous woman destroying the colony with her awesome fists and kicks. As she came near me, I got a bit tensed but kinda felt attracted and I said, "hello gorgeous stranger, care for a coffee, but I have to warn you that I'm married but if you come close to me I might go wild". She gave me a punch to my face!

I woke up with a fricking nose pain as if 200 bees stung on it. I saw my son smiling at me. Kinda put me in a deep thought, normally he would've been worried after something like this... but a smile. He started laughing but soon went silent as if.....

No, the dangerous aura came from behind me and what I saw.... it was haunted spirit from hell!! Worse! It was my haunted wife, she was looking bloodthirsty. My son went out of the room slowly step by step. The worst thing was that, she smelled like a disgusting rat. My mind was blank, why would she smell like a rat anyway. She hates rats, she is even afraid mice and pups which is her weak point. The smell was truly awfull. I kindly advised, “babe, you really need to take a bath”. As she lift her head slowly, I saw her face.

This is the end... My life has come to it’s dawn. I lived enough, may I rest in peace. God I’m coming..... As she came close to me, my heartbeat felt like it was running 200 miles per hour. She was going to murder me, why? I don’t know but as she came near me, I felt my end was near. The unexpected happened, she hugged me and broke down into tears. She was crying. I did not know what happened. Why was she crying a lot? I managed to calm her down after some ten minutes and gently wiped her tears. It was early evening

Before I could talk to her, she was already fast asleep. Yes, a truly abnormal kind of a wife. What else will I say? But what happened. I gently let her on the bed without making a sound. I went down to drink some water and I saw! Someone doing something! I thought that he was worried but no! He was playing games on his pc as if nothing ever happened. I got furious.

Kids these days have no feelings for their parents, not even bothered to check up on his parents, truly botherless. I went there at once without drinking water and when I reached there, he saw me and suddenly went back on home.I was about to give the traditional slap on his face and as he turned around, I felt sincere guilt. How could I? How could I even think of doing this. I can’t, I am not a good person. “It’s ok my boy, don’t fear me”. I soon cut to the chase.

“ What happened? Why was your mother in that mood?”

“Do you remember the gorgeous stranger that saved you from those huge rats?”

“Yes I do, why did she give a punch? I mean, I wasn’t rude, just asking her out”.

"It so happenes that the gorgeous stranger who saved you was mama, your wife?"

Everything was coming to light. Things slowy started to turn bright. As I digged in my thoughts, everything became clear but the fact that I did not recognise my wife but asked her out, gave me a tremendeous amount of fear.

I told my son to act as if nothing had happened. " what about the aweful rat smell?"

"A ....ah..."

"Just tell her that our dog Michael farted on her while she was asleep". I named my dog after my nemisis. Cute right?

After a while she was awake, I told her that she fainted while working and that he handled everything else. She hugged me tight in fear and said, "ra...ra...ra....rats!".

"No babe there are no rats near. It was all a bad dream".

"Then why do I smell rats?!"

"Just a while ago our dog farted on you. Nothing else".

"I will kick that dog out! You know that I hate dogs, I am a cat person but still I kept him because our son insisted. Where is the damn mutt, I am gonna kick that thing out!"

Once my wife takes a descision, not even the devil can control her. The dog is doomed. If my son finds out then he will hate me for life. I hugged her very tightly and said, "if it weren't the smell you would've never gave me a lovely hug. I hope this works (thats what I prayed). She blushed and said, "ok fine, I will excuse this awefull smell only this time."

My dog heard the entire conversation. I am pretty sure he understood my lie. He looked at me for a split second, I think he blinked the one eye at me. Good for me. My wife went down to the bathroom for a bath and saw our son playing games, so my wife went to him slowly and calmly. You might think that she would talk sweet but that ain't the reality, just because the father can't do the dirty work doesn't mean the mother can't. I immedaitely turned behind. Bam!! I heard a sound. I turned my back and just as I expected, my son was lying on the floor soundless.... knocked out cold. Indian mothers are always one of a kind.

As the year passed, the first few months were rough, I got rid of the rat infestation and cleaned the place. But the smell was a problem as if something had die. So we checked the entire place from top to bottom and what I found was literally life threatening.

My restaurant was not the rat colony but more like the rat graveyard. If this leaked out then, me and my restaurant both R.I.P. My restaurant will be sued by the Government and me? No, I have to stay positive and think calmly. My restaurant can still be a huge success, I just have to work this through. The next day, I hired the some experts and cleaned the entire place.

Ok, cleaning done and now, fixing. I went through the commercial stoves, they were filled with chucks of rust and dust which had accumulated over a period of time. The dishwasher was surprisingly still good, it still worked but it was dusty. The freezer was........... not that good, more like world war 2 safety bunker. Thank God, my previous staff always used to clean before leaving. The ingredients for the restaurant food were always fresh as the grocery supplier used to supply it to us every 2 days.

My restaurant had all the basic stuff and some of them were in a pretty good condition. Also the paint of the restaurant was starting to wear off. My restaurant, what have you become? Sure life plays tricks. A lot of money went in fixing the damage.

My wife started to go to a therapist. The reason was because she had a continous rat dream. I guess my wife was truly distraught and still in a bit of a shock. But even though she was afraid of rats, she still fought them to protect me. I guess I may have been a bad husband and neglected her most of the time. I have to focus more on her and my boy. They are my family. Even if this restaurant goes, my family will still be there with me and I know my wife and my son loves me a lot.

Okay, my restaurant is done. But there is one thing, I have to apologise to my wife. I indeed have caused a lot of trouble for her. Also, I had called the theapist, I told her everything. She was enjoying each and each every moment of my truth. I got angry and why wouldn't I? The therapist was laughing over the entire disscussion but I kept calm as it was my mistake as well.

Before I lost it, I hung up the phone. But that damn therapist called again. She apologised and informed me that my wife already knew about this but was not sure about it. I felt a lot of guilt as I lied to my own sweet wife.

I went home and I saw my boy Joseph playing games on his phone. I guess even if the world is coming to an end, then still he would play games without a worry. My boy is really naive but he will grow up to be a great person in life, only if his pc and mobile games stop but he understands his limits. He knows when to turn it off, he has full control. I saw the kichen door locked, kinda creepy. Never mind, I searched my wife and saw her in our garden, sitting peacefully.

It was a beautifull day filled with energy and air filled with the wonderfull fragrance of my garden flowers. There was my wife reading a book. I went closer and saw that she was reading a book about on how to get rid of nightmares..... I have to tell her the truth.

I told her each and everything, as she raised her hand I knew that I would wake up with a nose pain again but she hugged me instead and said,

"I am proud of the man you are and I will always love you no matter what"

Now I'm not a sentimental person but that actually was..... that felt great. I felt our relationship became stronger.

"Daddy, Mama dinner is ready".

"Lets go, today Joseph cooked". I was amazed, my son hardly comes to the kitchen anymore, i thought he got bored of cooking.

"Strange."

"What is it?"

"Joseph didn't let me into the kitchen the entire time. I hope he is not up to his pranks again".

I remembered that our kitchen door was locked, I didn't pay much attention but it seems his pranks will give me a heart attack today. By the time I reached, it was too late. I was going to die, atleast thats what I thought.

"Happy wedding anversary!!"

I looked at my wife and she looked at me, we both forgot. Kinda impressive how my son remembered. I looked at the food at the table. (shocked) My son's skills are better than me. Every dish was perfectly arranged, beautifully cooked. He even baked a huge cake. Either way, I have to taste check everyting.

It was perfect, each and every combination. The flavors burst in my mouth. My wife however, well she just stuffed the food in her mouth as if she was a hungry savage. Maybe she actually enjoyed the food. It was a beautifull dinner. My son later informed me that she did not eat much the entire week because of her thoughts about rats.... Oops.

The next day, we went to panjim to meet my parents and my in-laws, they too lived in panjim. At first, it was better to go to my in-laws because my parents are heavy talkers, not that I mind but.............lets just say I have family issues and the last time I went, it was a bloody verbal war between the both of us; father and son. I don't want my son to witness any more of that.

This time, the meet went kinda great, I met my in-laws. Both of them greeted me and my son Joseph as treasure. My wife on the other hand did not buy it, I guess she too had some family issues. My parents this time were also more appropriate and humble, especially my dad. He was more relaxed and calm. He even apologised infront of my wife and kids. I hugged my dad very tightly with a lot of affection and gratitude; my true and honest feelings. It takes real courage to appologise infront of everyone, I too apologised to him. It was a emotional moment for the both of us.

Later some time I went out alone to check my childhood friends. At this time of the hour, they will definitely be near the old football ground and I was absolutely correct. They were all pleased to meet me. But one was not among them. I asked about Antonio. They all said the same worls at the same time; 'drunked'.

I wouln't be surprised, in fact he is the greatest drunked around the entire place, even the kids know him as 'bhebdoh mama' (uncle drunked) and by the adults; 'Antonnio bhebdoh Fernandes'. Now, his story is completely whacked up in such a way that it is nearly impossible to belive.

Antonio Fernandes, the first person to be with if the world is coming to an end. Now why? Cause he is a womanizer and a bad drunked. I know he is a bad person but before becoming such a person, we promised each other that no matter what, friends forever.....brothers for life. Plus, he was always scared of my wife and my sister, so I never had any such problems.

Antonio was not always like this, his past was truly grusome. He was orginaly from a sweet village called Assolna. Assolna is usually known for restaurants, ferry, the small traditional market and local institutions. He had abusive parents who never bothered to care for him but however for attention, he would do anything his parents commanded him to do. He always was under the influence of his parents. He loved them but his parents....

His parents literally used to torture him, sometimes hitting him a lot and making him do bad deeds. One day, he realised everything, that enough was enough. He ran away from home and came to Panjim, the capital of Goa. It lies on the estuary of the Mandavi River. It is home to awesome colonial structures and with modern architecture. Quite the place for tourism and the perfect place for bussiness. But for Antonio it was the perfect place to live, away from all negativity and away from his parents.

I first met him on the ferry boat. I caught him red handed snucking on the boats and stealing money. When I caught his hand, I felt the flesh less and more of his bone. He was like a side character from a zombie movie. When the police came to arrest him, Salvador and I both decided to let him off. I had no problem with lying but Salvador was hesitant..... he belived in speaking ony the truth but for the sake of the poor being, he did the one thing that he never wanted to do, to lie.

We made up a lie saying that the pale fellow was actually our friend who had contracted HIV right from birth, from his parents and that his parents were dead and his poor uncle and aunt were taking care of him. Now, even a dumb person wouldn't buy this shit but the police actually bought all of it, in my surprise, they got emotional with tears in their eyes and we got off with a ten ruppee fine. Years ago the ten ruppees were a lot and we had been collecting money all year round to celebrate chritmass between us and it was the chritsmass day so..... me and Salvador gave it away. For Antonio, it was a christmass miracle, he not only got away but found two people who he can truly call as friends.

We gave a lot to Antonio, especially Salvador. Salvador literally begged his parents and grandparents along with all his uncles and aunts; the entire family, to let Antonio stay. After a 5 hours of continuous begging, they agreed. They had one condition, that Antonio will do all the chores of the house and they will not only give a place to stay but as well as pay for his education. That was enough, Antonio burst into tears, he never went to school so he was really happy and another great thing was that Salvodor's grandfather was the director general of police of Goa and his father was an inspector.

Antonio told each and everything, we all got emotional but Salvador's sister who was only 4 years old started clapping! This made me belive that she was cracked up, from that moment I always stayed away from her, to be honest I have a history with Salvador elder sister but that is for later. Thank God they accepted him, if they had not then I had to take him to my parents. My parents, forget begging, they would've kicked me out.

Life went on for Antonio, but his past always haunted him. He became a successfull man but an alcoholic and a womanizer along side. Till date, he is still single. The reason is......... he fell in love with a statue!!

One day he called the both of us saying that he found his soulmate. We felt like giving a huge celebration for him. We thought that we will meet her at a very lovely place but no. He took us to a church. We thought that maybe his girl is a prayerfull person. He introduced us to a statue of Mother Mary!!! Maybe he was kidding with us so we both laughed but he became serious, he said that he loved her and she was the women of his life. I smiled but I was shocked at the same time. What a twist? Salvador got furious.

"Aah!!!"

"If you wanted to become a priest, you could just have said so!!!". Screamed Salvador.

The priest heard his noise and gave him a verbal 2nd degree hammering. Oh God, I would've never survived such a scolding. In the end, we both talked to Antonio. We told him that such a thing is unethical and immoral. I just thought in my head for a while. If he truly fell for Mother Mary and married her then..........

In the end, Antonio had a breakup with the statue of Mother Mary but later on he never fell in love. So creepy....... maybe I still sometimes don't understand love. That's his story, whacked up right? Maybe he should've become a priest. Or just maybe he was mentally ill from his past abuse.

Later I went to search him. I knew exactly where he was, right at the beach house. I found him in the worst shape possible. He was lying naked with a bottle. I quickly called Salvador and told him everything. He at once came as if the world was coming to an end. Plus only a drunked understands another drunked. I wouldn't be surprised.

We both held him up and dressed him, then we woke him up. If we tell him that he was lying naked, the guy would obviously hate himself. Surprisingly, he doesn't hate himself for womanizing and drinking; his way of life. I guess being naked and losing a ton of money concerns my friend more. Salvador felt pity on him but me, I felt absolute rage. He is like a younger brother to me. All he does is drink and drink till his body won't take it.

After some while of being awake and sound, I left out all my rage of destruction on him. I scolded him so much, he fell unconscious. Just kidding, no he did not. Quite surprising, he took all my scoldings as if he was drinking coconut water. What was happening to him?.

"It's no use Joey. He has even gotten used to the verbal third degree combination of your parents scolding as well." Salvador exclaimed.

"What!!!" I myself will fall into a coma if that ever happened to me. I'm not joking, I'm serious. This guy had become the ultimate being of pure mental strength. With this, I was absolutely sure that even the greatest of the greatest mentally strong people were like ants to him; they could only bite but this guy, would crush them.

We went to our favourite beach restaurant, 'golden fish' to have something. It had become a beautifull place. Fully refurbished, absolute perfection. I called wife and informed her that I won't be there for lunch. Her reply was,

"If you can't spend time with your family, then go to hell!!"

Oh God, a lot is happening in my life. Salvador too informed Maria that he won't be able to make in time for lunch. I knew he was going to get hammering. Shockingly, the opposite happened. He got off with it..... why do such things happen to me alone God?

We were trying to convince Antonio for his good being..... and right at that moment we saw a beautiful woman smilling at Antonio passing by. It was a potuguese woman who seemed to be around her late thirtees.

"Now's my chance". Antonio left, like a wind desiring to touch a beautifull flower.

"Salvador, what do you think?"

"Nothing but our fellow will never learn his lesson".

"No! Thats not what I asked you. Will he succeed?"

"Definitely, he has the looks and skills needed for the job. Uptill now, no woman has ever been able to resist him."

"Yeah, you're right. It would be a miracle if the woman says no."

Life is full of twists and turns. The miracle happened, the woman grew furious of him. She punched Antonio in the face. He at once fell from the chair dragging the table cloth on him.

"The next time you talk to a lady, you better have some manners!!"

"Ye...ye...yes mam." Antonio in fear.

The woman left and everyone started laughing at him but he was still, sitting on the floor, he looked as if he was day dreaming. Salvador went and picked him up. He lift up Antonio and tidied the table as a decent fellow would do and brought him back to our table. I was fed up with Antonio, I was pretty sure that he was still not ready to learn his lesson. He did take verbal third degree from my parents.

"She is the one". Antonio said, with confidence.

"What ?" Salvador in shock.

"Really?" me being happy. Finally he found someone.

"Yes, she is the one for me. I will definitely marry her you guys see."

He was one hundred percent sure. Me and Salvador looked at each other, we burst into laughter.

"What's wrong, you guys think that I might fail?"

"No." We both said. He just didn't know what he was putting his life into. Me and Salvador are not bad people but ours wives are somewhat similar to that woman so....... his life will be a living hell on earth but on the other hand, the woman is perfect for him. she will definitely get his ass back to line.

"No, she is perfect for you." I said. Salvador also shaked his head yes.

"Then it's decided. I will marry her no matter what."

After a while of having food, discussing life problems and refreshing old memories, we finally decided to leave and I had to go, cause if I don't reach in time, than my wife and my parents combined scolding will give me tortureful nightmares for the rest of my life. Just as we were about to leave, Salvador stopped me.

"Joey wait!"

"What is it, I have to go".

"Do you care that less for our brother." Now, his words made deep sense. We know nothing about the woman, what if she is not a good person. There are many people in todays society who show that they are good but they can be rotten to the core.

“We can’t just leave Antonio like that. What if the woman is bad?” Salvador really caught my attention.

We went back into the restaurant and met with the owner. The 82 year old recognised us at first glance, he was handling the restaurant for more than forty years.

“The two boys have finally come back to pay me a visit.” Filled with excitement after seeing us after some time.

“I hope you guys are doing good in life” wow, he is still healthy and that to smoking a cigar.....doesn’t smoking kills?

“Yes we are.” Salvador replied with a smile.

“Please sit for a while. Have something. If it weren’t you both guys then my restaurant would have been dead long time ago.”

Looking back at our favourite restaurant; ‘golden fish’, it was quite different years ago. It has it’s bad history. Back when the restaurant started before I was even born, it was becoming successfull and gaining fame at a normal pace but at the time of my glory days, the quality of the food served here was worse. People even found a huge dead cockroach in the kitchen. The chefs were all disgusting and the owner lost faith and spirit in his restaurant.

Me and Salvador wanted to save the place from becoming a ruin so me and Salvador went to the owner and made him a deal. The deal was simple, we both would use the place for two years and the owner will get 80% of the profit every month. Yh, somewhat charity to the place....we just loved the place. The owner who lost all faith saw a glimmer of hope in both of us. He agreed to the deal and we made the contract.

We at once fired the entire staff. We called all our old classmates who were perfect cooks, plus they were jobless so..... it worked pretty well, some agreed and some did not. Their reason was quite simple they didn’t like the bad reputation the restaurant had. Actually I could make out that it was more of an excuse as when I first asked them, they agreed but when I talked about their low salaries they........... forget about it, at least I have the ones who agreed. I gave them multiple reasons on why they shouldn’t join. Their reply was simple but fricking smart. They said that they wanted their skills to be of use. For Salvador it was creepy, all who agreed said the same exact words. There is nothing creepy in it, isn't?

We all came together. We cleaned the place first, we left no untidy spots. One of our staff memebers found a pink underwear in the restroom. Whose was it? The old staff was full of shit. We found a lot of stuff. Treasure for perverts and disgusting mess for all of us. Who keeps a porn magazine beneath the kitchen drawers. This is place to cook, oh God!!

We cleaned each and everything. We checked all the kitchen epquipments, they were all in good shape. We sent out posters to each and everyone around the area. It was a huge success, for the two years the restaurants bloomed. Sure we had many problems due to shortage of food. Lets say everyone loved our food so much that the restaurant finally start to shine again.

At the end of the two year contract, some left as they had enough experience and I kept someone suitable to handle the restaurant, there were some newcomeres also so the restaurant lacked nothing. The owner cried tears of joy. He was truly filled with contentment. He was a bit sad as we left the restaurant. Me and Salvador both kept a very good name of this restaurant. Our parents were the proudest of all, I was a bit angry on mine. They said that I would fail badly and that I would get bankrupt and loose everthing. Just because I became a hero of the restaurant, they changed just to say that the golden fish restaurant saviour, is my son. But nevermind.

Back to the current time,

"Could we just meet Francis?"

"Sure but please have something".

"We already ate at your restaurant. It was quite good".

"ok, Francis! Where are you? Look who came to meet you".

"Coming Mr.John"

Francis never left the restaurant, at times he was the waiter and when needed, a cook too.

"Oh boys! How have you guys been? I hope you'll are doing just fine."

"Yeah we are, what about you?"

"Same old, same old"

"We were just curious about the woman who punched Antonio down to the ground."

"That boy Antonio never learns, he maybe rich but he is still lagging in his life." The owner comented.

"Yes, but after he recieved a punch from that lady, he immediately fell in love." Salvador had to say.

"And thats the reason we wanted to know about her, if she is a good woman or not."

"Who Diana?" she is good person, no need to worry.

" what? That rascal is after my granddaughter, I will never allow it." The owner was furious.

Why did I forget that the owner was portuguese ? It seems Antonio is in big trouble.

It turns out that her parents died from a grusome car accident and that his grandson and granddaughter was brought to Goa since they were little , they needed care. They were planing to leave Goa but due to the pandemic they stayed and promised their grandparents that they won't leave unless the pandemic ends. Don't they love their grandparents too much? Too good to be true. I guess Antonio is set. This is one of the positive effects of the pandemic, if the woman had left then Antonio would be single until his next life.....was pretty sure of it.

Before leaving, the owner; Mr.John gave us take way food. It was fish salad, my wife's favourite. Thanfully she will let me off. I arrived, thankfully my wife did not scoled me, neither my parents but my son did. Why? Why is my life as such God? Not from my boy! This is torture!!

Before leaving, I even met my sister, my wife was not happy to see her. Why don't they like each other? Some hidden past I guess. I asked Salvador, if he had any clue. What he told me was quite annoying but true, my wife and my sister are such. It turned out that they used to be good friends at the martial arts club but they fought for a beautifull cat. They even traded fists and kicks, which were so hard that they ended up killing the cat by mistake, who was caught in between. I asked him on about how he knew.

His response convinced me that my sister never really grew up. He told me, "I just get her drunk and make her play the game of truth and dare." Now I felt like punching Salvador in the face for that but........ he is my best friend and thats one smart way. So you can say, that I was actually impressed.

I went back to my place and reached at around 3.00 PM, it was a long tiring journey. A lot had happened in just one visit.

CHAPTER FOUR

Life Is Innocent

Months passed, life had started to become steady. Tourism slowly started to revive in Goa. My restaurant had finally started to go well. In the past few weeks I finally managed to get some pro cooks for my place. Life slowly started to grow again. Sure, it was tough for some but they too managed to finally catch up.

My son on the other place slowing started to make some progress, or so he says. He failed in mathematics in the first two exams and said that he did not intend to study. My son, why? Why has he changed? His future sometimes concerns me. He says he is fine, maybe he has done some progress.

After some few days, my son comes and tells me the most exciting news, but it was a shock for my wife. It turned out that he finally found a girlfriend, I was glad for my boy but his mother........... was not.

"You failed in your exams and you dare to find a girlfriend!!"

"But mama, I never proposed to her. She proposed to me!!"

"How can that happen ? I am definitely sure that she is a gold digger."

"How?" My son in shock.

"Because! Now's not the time to do such stuff."

My son and wife's fight did not bother me. Infact, I was in my old flashbacks. The day that I proposed to my Sana. Sure Michael was my nemisis back then but he still helped a lot that day. That day, I still remember it as it was yesterday, I was 27 years old. No, it did not go as I planned but still, I got the person who I desired the most, to spend the rest of my life with; my Sana.

That day Salvador and my sister were out on a date. Sana and me decided to go for a picnic to Colva. Colva back was not how it is today. There were lushy green fields everywhere, near the church and infront as well. A peacefull place to be, people were diffident and also full of kindness. The beach was so exotic,cool and the perfect place to propose our love.

Sure, sometimes there was a crowd, but never used to bother others. Most of us Goans used to work on ships and even today. During the evening it was the best. The sun set by the golden sand looked fabulous and I still does but people litter the place in these days. To live in Colva, life was full of peace. Sure, there was some tourism but it was steady and just blooming. The best fish market was in Colva, just next to the beach where many women and few men used to sell fresh fish. Most of the men used to do fishing. Tourism activities was very less.

There is a festival that takes place every year. All the Goans never miss it and it takes pace only in Colva. It's the Colva Fama also know as the 'Feast of Menino (infant) Jesus'. The Colva Fama till now, has been celebrated for four centuries. What happened? Why do they celebrate it? There is very special story to it.

Accpording to a 17th century legend, a jesuit priest and a sailor, priest Benito Fereirra, found the statue on the coast off Mozambique. The priest brought the statue along with him when he got posted to 'Our Lady of Mercy' church in Colva, Goa. Even since the priest kept in on the altar, miracles began to happen. But when he got transferred to the Rachol seminary, he took the statue with him. the villagers begged him to hand the staue to them but he refused. In disapiontment, the villagers made their way back. On their return journey, they found a diamond ring, it was the same ring that was on the finger on Infant jesus's statue. They rejoyced, went back and another replica of the statue and put the ring on it's finger.

I do not know what exactly happened as there is another legend. A long time ago, could be during the poruguese rule, the fishermen who were occupied in their fishing, saw a huge flock of sea gulls, hovering over the ocean. Something was shining. Thinking that it maybe someone signally for help, the fishermen quickly aproached and found a gorgeous wooden carved idol of a baby with a hoop on it's finger.

They removed it and was later identified as the image of infant Jesus and initiated veneration. There were many claims that the image was miraculus and cured many people's diseases. This let to it's fame spreading entire Goa. The crowds began to swell which led to the celebration of fama.

Kinda weird. In both the legends, someone or some people found something in the river or the ocean, but people never question, maybe people only wish to live on.

Anyway, back to the part, I took Sana to Colva and no, I was not wealthy to buy a ring. Even though my cooking skills were awesome, I was still poor. Nowadays, everyone buys a ring, it has become a tradition or a custom to present a beautiful but an expensive ring to the woman who men dersire to marry. Sana was also poor, even though she worked her way up through education, she was still trying to find a job.

Coming to Colva for picnic was the best descision of our lives. It was the perfect day of our lives, I proposed to her in the most awesome way possible. Let me explain, at first when we reached colva, I found Michael sitting in a restaurant, it seemed that he was on a date. We both met each other by mistake. The waiter who was serving food switched our foods where the table Michael and his date was. We both complained at the time. That is when we experienced that our worlds were about to crash with each other.

When I saw the face of the girl who was dating with him, it was Salvador's elder sister, Aurora........ my ex crush. I fainted, Salvador is dating my sister and his sister is dating Michael.

"No! I don't want to be related with this guy!" I woke up screaming these words, in the Hospicio hospital which was in Margao.

"Don't shout you dummy, we're in a hospital." Sana was furious.

"No I just had the weird dream!"

"What dream?"

I sawtwo people coming inside to meet me, it was not a dream. It was the reality! Aurora explained herself, it seems that they had just decided to get married. She raised her hand and on her finger, a diamond ring. If I do remember, I did proposed to her once but she denied......it was before I found Sana. Her reason was simple, she stated that I was too poor and she did not like poor people. What a golddigger, right?

My Sana got jealous, she looked at me in furious eyes when saw the diamond ring and I felt disappionted. True, I was really poor, actually jobless. I thought that maybe he had a high paying job or actually owned a bussiness. No, I was wrong. He actually bought the ring with his parents money. His parents were super rich if I remember. They always used to look down on poor people. I asked about his job and his reply was that he was an advocate who was not earning much, but will inherited his parents fortune for himself and for Aurora.

Sana looked at me with a proud look in her eyes. She was proud because I was not like Michael. She wispered, "I rather accept the you who is poor, than the you who will depend on his parents fortune."

After listening to her words, the most important words for our lives just came out as slippery as butter, I could'nt controlled those words, " will you marry me?".

Michael and Aurora were shocked but Sana on the other hand was deeply content after hearing those words and she said, "yes." We kissed, not going to lie. Both of them started laughing at us, "poor people will always marry other poor people." Well, who's poor now, I am far more richer than him!

Sana got angry, she decided to beat both of them up for the real good. Looking at Sana's about to burst rage, Michael and Aurora ran away. We on the other hand were really happy.just when I was getting dispatched from the hospital, I came the day's newspaper. I read that an experienced cook was needed at a restaurant which had just started. I just showed it to Sana, instead of reading the stuff that I had just found out, she read a job which was perfect according to her qualifications. We both looked at each other. Life was set, we had already decided. We were going to take the job.So wait............. is this what they call God's plan and also the outcome of my descisions?

In just one year after getting accepted, we decided that we would marry each other and settle in Colva. Due to our financial situation, we decided not to have kids at the moment. So it all worked, due to my wife's excellent performance, she got promoted a lot and me after collecting money I had finally decided to open my own restaurant and then my boy Joseph was born, then everything went smooth. It took some few years but Ifinally did it on my own knees together with my wife's efforts also.

At the current situation, the fight. Oh God. Both mother and son will continue to fight if I don't think of a solution.

It is the modern era, we have to solve our problems in a positive way. "Why don't you test the girl Sana?" just to stop these fights.

"Fine, I will....."

Oh, she definetly had a plan. I too went through the same thing when I told my parents about marrying Sana. My father was on good terms and wanted to meet the woman of my life but my mother, well......... she had something in her mind. Anyways, Sana passed with a high score from my mother.

Some few days had passed, it was a Sunday. My boy was going out. I thought my wife was going with him to check the girl but she did not. I did not know what was going on. My wife is letting my boy go out with his first girlfriend. What was happening?

"All the best." Mother to son.

"Thank you madaam." Son to mother.

What in the blue heck was happening ? Sudden change! Why? Oh God, please help me for I am losing my sanity. Is this a dream?

"Now what's wrong? Why are you day dreaming?"

"Day dreaming and me, no."

"Then why do you look so puzzeled ?"

"Puzzeled? Just a few days ago you were against him going out with a girl and now you are letting him off ?"

"You really think I'm a bad mother, who will keep our son locked in home prison?"

"Yes!! Wait......I meant to say no!" why was I hesitating?

"What's wrong with you!! Why are you being such a sus?" (angered wife).

"Nothing, it's just that...that......I'm really confused. What is happening."

"You na, always confused. Listen, I told him to take his girlfriend out to the beach, to spend some time with each other. During the date he will make an excuse to grab her phone and check her contact list, that all."

"I still didn't understand............what dish are you cooking Sana?"

"Oh today, I'm cooking chicken 65." Idiotic wife.

"Oh ! 4th grade english text book ! I'm asking you, what are you planning with this, what will our boy get?"

"You just wait. Let our boy come home, everthing will be crystal clear."

These ladies in these days are too smart yet idiotic. I just pray if her planing turns out better then her chicken 65. The day went on, it was evening and my son came with a relived but a tiring look. Did something happen?

"Mama, you were right.That girl is a golddigger."

"See, I told you."

What was happening ? My wife looked very proud. What did happened ? I looked at my wife with utter disbelief and my face was a question mark.

"Sana, what did happen ? why are looking so proud and what did he mean?"

"You duffer, never really grew up !"

"I'm going for a shower !"

"First let him take the shower. Once he comes, he will tell you everything." My wife is giving me thriller for the day. As if.....

"Ok fine." I noded.

I wonder what mother and son cooked together. I just hope that it's something good. I sometimes feel as if my life is a novel and an author is writing it. Eh, it's just a feeling.

Suddenly my phone rang, it was Antonio's. I picked it up and......

"Joey I want help !"

"What happened ?"

"It's Diana ! she....."

"What happened to her ! Don't tell you got her pregnant!"

"No! if I get opportunity I'd be more than happy."

"Then my saint Antonio, what happened ?"

"Well she.......she........ she friendzoned me!"

When I those heard words I almost got a stroke due to my intensive anger. My God, this guy should be happy, at least he managed to get step one. But he is shocked because he got friendzoned. Let me mess him up more, I will give him a good one. He should'nt troubled me like this !

"You bum ! what did you do to make her friendzone you. Oh no, this is a very bad sign. What have you done ? you have ruined yourself."

"What should I do ? she even said that she always wanted a younger brother to play with and her elder brother does not bother about and that I am like a ounger brother to her !"

Oh, so he got bro zoned......very good. He deserves it for wasting my time.

"Listen to me, there are many girls in this world. Don't worry be happy. You wanted to get into a relationship na, so now you got."

"Please don't say that, I know she is the one. Aren't I like your brother ?"

"Brother in arms is what he means but thats a story for another time."

"See ....! you manged step one. It means she has begun to trust you, if you truly want her then you shall get her, happy?"

"Thank you! love you man." He needs to get his brain checked.

Soon after I kept the phone my son came and sat on the sofa. I asked about his date and he said,

"Daddy, there are fake people in this world."

"I did not understand you, what do you mean?"

He just looks down and keeps quite, I was getting anxious. Then I looked at my wife and she was staring at me with furiosity, I then understood. My wife explained later that the girl was not a good person and that our son had to dump her. The plan went like this, he asked for her phone to click some photos and mean while went through her personal stuff.......turned out she had three more boyfriends...wow. She's a player....

Hm..... when I too was growing up through my teen years, I used to get all of that everytime but this was my son's first time. It truly must've shocked him, well he is still in the process of getting out of his bubble. He is innocent of course and to be honest, the Goan thinking of having a girlfriend at this age is not supported.

My son's life is beautiful, it's how he makes his life. Right now, he is sad but one day he will meet someone amazing. Our destiny is always in our hands. For now he is very naive but he learns from his mistakes. You should not stop a child from commiting mistakes but instead you should correct them after they commit mistakes.

CHAPTER FIVE

The Calm Wave

Christmass went by but only a few celebrating it, it is tradition to light up our houses with decorations and colourful lights but only a few including me put ‘em. People went through a lot.

The new year 2021 began with high hopes, my son was mentaly ready to ace his exams, yh..... only mentaly. Wonder when will he truly grow up. He kept on failing in maths. I had enough and made him join tuitions forcefully. Since then, he has been quite a student.

My wife like always resumed her work. By now everyone had adapted to the pandemic, everyone was used to wearing a mask. My resatuarant bloomed once again, people started coming back although they were not all foreign tourists but most were indian travelers. I was was a bit content but not entirely.

I am a bussinessman, I desire more profit. Of course, life as a househusband was fun but not easy and non- profitable in terms of finance. People may take life as a cruel joke and laugh it off but not me. I instead make sick jokes on life and then I take it seriously. In short, I can be the best bussinessman of all time if I push myself to the limit not stay in the same place. Life is about change, when it is needed not desired. Life is definity about growth as it is needed and desired at the same time.

The year went t by like a normal one with the pandemic with sudden climate change. Most of the year, it rained in Goa. For some it was sivering but for me, profitable. Due to the cold rainy weather, people would literally come out and go frequently to restaurants and mine served the best food of all so...... my restaurant shinned double.

April 21st 2021. Late at night, it was around 11 or 11.12 PM than Salvador gave a phone call. I didn't waste time, I got up, woke Joseph and Sana immediately. I turned on the ignition, took the car on the road and went for panjim with my wife and kid. I explained everything to them while driving on the road.

My sister fell very sick, she had suddenly contracted pneumonia. I at once went to the hospital to see her, everyone excluding Salvador was not there which was shocking.......wasn't he the one who called me. I saw her in the ICU and she was in the worst state.

I saw Edward standing next to my mother, I asked about Salvador and he said, "right behind you." What the hell!! He gave me a heartache, the guy ran so fast behind me. He at once gave a bag to the docter. It seems that the staff ran out of supplies. After a while the docter informed us that she needs rest and is safe.

I asked Salvador what exactly happened. He said,

"She had stopped drinking wine and liquor for a month." What in the blue heck! Who gets pneumonia by not drinking?

"Listen, did she eat too much ice-cream this entire month?"

"How did you know?" he really needs to grow up.

"Wait, people don't get pneumonia by eating ice-ceam." Yh.....tell that to the ice that reaches down to the stomach, not a good one. Plus we don't know the stuff is healthy made or not. Just kidding.

"Forget about it." I ended the hot topic right then. She is safe that is all that matters.

I took a look at Edward. Its been three years since the last time I saw him, he looked really pale and weak. It turned out that Edward came alone, I knew something was wrong. Salvador too noticed this and we both decided to talk to him. I asked Salvador about his son, it turned out he was doing quite well. His son is quite adaptable, he is getting good results and plus, he studying abroad.

"Hey Edward, how have you been doing?" Salvador initiated the conversation.

"I don't know." With a depressed tone.

He broke down in tears.

"My marriage is over, my kids don't love me anymore."

From my little brothers words, I knew his life got messed up. Years ago when my mother was trying to find the best woman for my brother, someone informed her of a young and a beautiful women that would fit the descriptions. What my mother didn't know was that the woman never wanted the marriage with my brother and loved some other guy. Those were the rumors that I heard and I even heard that she was being forced to marry my brother as he did have better income and money in his pockets.

I had informed all of this to my mother. To which she replied, "people will simply say whatever they want and I asked the girl personally. She said that she had no problem, she seemed such a kind and a humble person."

I even told my dad but he was least bothered, for him his word was important. Times have not completely changed, people even today get married against their own will and their lives get destroyed. My brother was in a condition as such, the woman didn't want to marry my brother and was caught up in this mess. He too had someone who he loved but my parents never excepted his love due to some reasons.

I calmed my brother down, my parents too were sad for him. what could be done, everything had already happened and it can't be undone. I asked him of the entire story and told me that for years she was having an affair with some guy and that his kids were not actually his. My brother was a victim, he did not deserve this. I did not ask him anything else, he was in too much pain nor did I ask him how he found out.

A lot of stuff happened to people during the begining of the pandemic, some people got good, some got bad and some got the worst. People went through a lot.

The next day my sister woke up. She felt great, thats what she said. After some few months, she finally got the news about Edward. She was quite calm....... This meant a huge tsunami was on it's way. At this age Goan women become fat but my sister was still in shape after all these years. Edward had moved back in with my parents some months ago. Maria called all the family members to the house where Edward first lived and this time she called my wife for help. My wife did not hesitate to say yes.

That day the two women showcased their combined brute power. They both went and infront of the entire colony gave a brute beating to woman and her boyfriend (**the female gladiators**). Hell, humiliation as well as a beating. Beating from the female brutes. It was awesome! My son and I enoyed a lot. Listen, I don't encourage voilence but this was awesome. Sure the police came, everyone in the colony supported us and my wife with my sister were left off with a warning. Now, I feel bad for what happened, she too was married against her own will but she should have informed Edward before marriage, I understand this. Plus she was not kept as a prisoner at her house that time........hehehe.....Edward had a good time and his kids well.....they went to take Edwards side, even though he may not be their actual father but they except each other and thats more than enough.

A lot of crazy stuff has happened therin after, the fear of the pandemic has started to wear off, people have finally adapted. We humans are moving on, sure it's not entirly over but we learned a lot; how to live proper, spending time with your loved ones and growing yourself to further improvement.

I have a crazy wild family, also a crazy life. Well, I thank God in everyway possible. Each and every journey is a blessing, we experience and learn a lot .

9 798887 172880

Printed by Libri Plureos GmbH in Hamburg,
Germany